GW00713156

As if the Rain
Fell in Ordinary Time

P. D. Lyons

**Winner of the 2019 erbacce-prize for poetry
from eight thousand submissions world-wide**

WESTMEATH COUNTY COUNCIL
Comhairle Chontae na hIarmhí

erbacce-press
Liverpool UK

To
Flora Rosano-Lyons & Donald R. Lyons
Thank you, as always, for the gift.

Acknowledgements

Some of these poems have previously appeared in public. The poet is grateful to the editors of these publications for their kind support and permission to include the pieces here.

Inquietudes Literary Journal, Lapwing Press, Subterranean Blue Poetry, erbacce-press, West 47 Galway Arts, A New Ulster, Virtual Writer Longford, Thunderclap, Dimensions Magazine, Eleutheria Scottish Poetry Review, Calliope Nerve, Danse Macabre, Vox Poetica, Fresh Ink NVCC, Cuirt Annual Galway, Yes Factory, Right Hand Pointing, In Protest: New Human Rights Poetry – and all those others throughout the years; who said yes!

Also:

...the author would like to express a deep appreciation for all the efforts of the entire *erbacce* crew on making this book a possiblity, especially Dr. Alan Corkish; cheers mate!

Contents:

Waltzing the Night

holding ourselves like prayers between each other
all summer sway cool tall screened windows
bright sound crickets fireflies glimmer
bare feet, beating hearts
soft by each other's breath
accented full moon kisses
beyond any daytime horizon…

~

it was one o'clock this morning.
woke up no reason
kitchen floor so cold I hurt for shoes
stood there adjusting to Frigidaire light
three bottles of beer on the second shelf
opened one by the window
chugged away to those long
hard rain halos

it's not the city I used to know with you

maybe I go for another
maybe it'll help me sleep
probably not
these days once I'm up
even beer can't touch me
deserted by even the small comfort of your ghost
still I sway as if somehow
we're dancing

Promised Land

14 stories up
Sometime after all the twilight zones had ended
Crane my head twin tower view.
 Count all the windows I could see that held a light

Another smoke
Watch across the west side highway for freighters
Illumination not of a land locked sort proving an Island after all.

I could not help the way we burned through our time together
 How hungry I was
How urgent that you be hungrier.
We left it spinning, the world we knew
Our ragged selves
Cities of our hearts
Wilderness of our bodies
Ghosts of unborn children
Smoke cross the promised land -
What could we give that had not passed?

There was that old Pontiac
 Yellow primer Firebird.
 Day into the drink already.
Gonna drive to the city.
You said you had to pee first.
OK. Parked at the mall.
You kicked open the door, got out
Instead of going in squatted right there.
Deluge beats over the black top.

 Got in a row over that.
For some reason it really pissed me off.
Then in ever escalation you said something.
Whatever it was it made me so sorry for yelling.
I hugged you, cried all over you.

We got better after that.
Dried off, had a smoke.
Then I drove.

Today you want to see Priscilla

She lives two blocks up
from where you have to live with your father
because Priscilla is crazy, and you couldn't
stay with her.

Priscilla makes her money from the cards. But
whenever you ask her to read yours, she always says
she knows you too well and that knowledge
clouds her wisdom.

You want to go up to her today, watching from
her cool back room through a crack in the door -
Priscilla, her rich fingers fat with bands of gold and sparkling stones
spreading cards by candlelight
speaking to some stranger in that different kind of voice even you
would hardly know.

You're on your way but then Carey has himself a dollar
So, the afternoon gets spent at Daz's where pin ball's still a dime
and sometimes you play good enough to pop for extra games

Something in the Night

back then when knowing the night was an obligation
I got to meet you
we had nothing to do but each other
we had no one else we wanted to bother with

I was working at a local gas station
 pump the gas, check the oil, fill the radiator, fill the tire
 only other things we could sell - cigarettes, maps and coca cola.
I have no idea what you did something textile?
Bobbins, threads, piece work, bonus

somehow, we had met and that was all that mattered.
we liked to drive around at night,
few beers, couple packs of smokes, FM radio.
didn't go to bars much, drinking there cost more
besides we both had this inability to not piss people off.

last time we were in a bar?
this old Irish guy, the owner, liked you at first
gave you your third drink on the house
but when he was playing pool, money on the table
you kept grabbing the back of the cue just as he shot.

by the third time it wasn't funny, except to you.
few of the regulars told me; Better get her out of here. Now!
So, I did.

we stopped off in the middle of the intersection by St. Joseph's
cemetery smoking, talking, kissing - more than kissing.
never a soul, not even the cops came by to bother us.
we had some incredible luck when it came to it.

I told you what my favourite breakfast was.
so, you invited me one morning, your mother's house,
eggs Benedict you made yourself just for me.

I met your little brother then.
he was 7 maybe 10. He asked if I ever went fishing?
sure, when I was your age my dad used to always take me.
must a said I'd take him sometime
cause about a week after we stopped seeing each other
I get this phone call
could we go? maybe tomorrow? you know fishing?
I don't remember how but I told him no. It made me feel sad.
I knew what it was like to believe you were going fishing then not.

And you? Even if you were around, I don't think there's anything
here you wouldn't have already known and forgotten long ago.

Lessons on Foreign Languages in a Reeperbahn Café

Trees or torture...
My breasts were made for children and your hands
Choices are limited by the boundaries of the playing surface
How do you know that's not a table?
 We could meet in Ireland by the palm trees.
Everyone drinks Guinness and whiskey, everyone drinks Paddy
Even in the ancient holes of Greece, the big dig and who
wouldn't give up school for the bones of Archimedes?
To find the way past childhood, finding the past of childhood,
the paths of childhood past the personal to the collective...
Who wouldn't give up tomorrow for a chance to come into
Pandora's Box?
Well when I am god, I shall bless Pandora, bless Eve,
bless all those who
turned away from paradise, instead followed the stars.
Why? Why everything? Why not something else?
Ignorance may be bliss but consciousness divine...

...but if I could meet you in Ireland by the palm trees
yes, even I would drink Paddy whiskey with you from the bones
of Pandora's ass; and we could trace the historic exile of
our childhood to the music of Springsteen's: *Point
Blank, The Price You Pay, Ties that Bind*, as it tins through
some battery cassette. So, roll up another cigarette and pass
the Pandora but first let me see your eyes,
Let me lay my tongue on yours.
Let us swallow some of each other's spit,
like a Red Indian blood-brother ceremony and
yes, you can be Winnetou if you want to...

When I was in Greece I lived on dirt. No not even dirt but
sand – dust. The dust of hot sun and cruel fate, the dust of
ancient tombs split open like over-ripe fruit covered
everything with a resin crust. We were fond of bones and
murders, sacrifices, lesbians, our Spartan

swords and sleeping children. We hated columns and
Parthenons. Sweated ouzo and goat fat and when we farted
little black olives rolled down and out of our pant legs.

When I was in Europe I lived on sleep. I slept for days in
Wien, Vienna, Vienne, Vienna. Slept for Beethoven at his
tomb and at his little Platz by the statue near the
Shubert ring. I was frozen in the Maria Theresian Natural
History Museum – lost among stuffed and pickled corpses
of every creature known to man.
In Hamburg, the whole city is made of sleep. Sleep like a
giant smog impregnated everything and every moment. Its
embryonic motion grown heavy in a damp heat, like breath on
a still winter night of North Sea drifting downward with
hunger, for those German girls, who with the slenderness of
a homosexual fantasy covered me in the slick semen of their
love. Mouths moaning with love, cunts hungry
with love, assholes a dream of love…

In the states I lived on flesh. The flesh of pigs.
 Flesh of Ronald McDonald. Catholic flesh of Christ, bloodless
white and sour. I lived with the flesh of dead dogs, aborted infants;
sucked juices from the fresh wounds of teenage girls down
in the darkness of their daddy's garages. Dracula had nothing on
me man.
I walked the ninety-degree heats of New York City streets.
Streets made of skin and muscle like some giant souvenir of
Auschwitz.
 Tattoos sweating black ink and muggers.
Whenever I couldn't buy anything to eat all I had to do was lick the
street –
Meat Street USA. And when I could afford to bribe my way out to
the countryside? It was for a breath of fresh blood with a
little something still warm from its own body heat to chew on.

… But now we sit by the palm trees of Ireland
 our harps hung up to dry. Pandora's ass so dry, is

like a sponge sucking up Irish whiskey the way a drowning
man, sucks sea. We don't sleep any more. The only flesh we
eat is our own. You have met me here have taken the blood
of my wound into your own.
So, my dearest look at me; you have the saddest eyes I have ever known.
Do you remember the peace I stole from you in Hamburg years ago?
Now there is nothing to heal, nothing, no reason to
steal. So, roll up another cigarette. But first let me lay my tongue upon
yours, let my tongue sleep awhile in that sweet hole. Let
us see how long we can stay still like that and yes, you can be Winnetou
if you want to.

(for Cordula)

Once while I was away

You might have come
Expecting awkward greeting won by
Philosophic well-planned answers to
What you thought my unasked questions were -
Accidental touch
Silent linger hands
Knowing prelude to a kiss
   All it would take to unclench my heart
   Inviting you in
   So, you'd have something to do for the afternoon

Pensioners Remiss

When I wanted to see you,
Young and available
Dresses out amidst a blue jean wasteland
Stoned as laughter smoky charms
Dancing any moment unannounced

On the steps of Spanish little Harlem
Turquoise as your eyes church doors
Sacramental wine just opened
A spiral of possibilities each as believable as the past.

When I wanted to see you,
Roads wide open looking to ride
Strong summer muscles
 Love like horses into sunset.

 Diamonds across that midnight sky
 Alive only in your love me eyes.
Breathless barefoot pirouette
 Limitless kitchens, dull Frigidaire light.
 Icy India Pale Ale fast as you can drink.
 Third floor back porch dawn
Aegean blue amongst a city of fearlessness.

When I wanted to see you,
Saint John's Chapel Christmas
 Balsam crushed blood velvet
Crystal choir angel
Mysterious as snow.
The mouth you used an accent of hypnosis
Lead like sorrow obsessed with green
 As if summer returned between live pines
 My hands held by your own to cup each one instead.

When I wanted to see you,
So much more so than wherever you were
Sharper than anything ever dreamed
So much sooner than now.

Knowing now the healing ways

I could touch you then. I knew you, just around the corner you.
Halfway Up the stairs, you. A single rose growing between back
yard rubble, you. Travelled by Grey Hound, cross the country,
park bench dreamer, double dancer Zelda, you -

A tide of whirlpools. An antebellum majorette beauty queen.
You were the most beautiful woman in the world. You were me
as a woman. Wanting to be the first one to make love in a whole
summer of dry attics never believing for one minute we could
end up on the street by Christmas in Connecticut.

I was gonna. I was destined. I was the one. I was the chosen.
Could have been Jesus, preferred to be Krishna, hoped only to
be Watermelon Sugar. A thing delectable to your lips, a thing
you might someday remember without lying or regret.

You were anything possible,
Meeting again someday.
Around the corner, halfway up the stairs,
Eyes still same as my own,
Knowing now the healing ways,
Strong enough for love.

Atlantic Luncheonette

I walked out into a morning
too bright against my shadows.
Three steps down I'm on the pavement
wondering just how able I am to get along -
Stable as loose change,
balanced as a junkie on the prowl.
Still can't stop thinking about moving
where it is, I'll finally get to.
My boots are holes turning into blisters.
Cigarettes keep tempting me with immortality.
Girls across the street dare me to smile.

I make up excuses to call what I'm eating food.
The waitress sings to the radio
with commercial interruption asks how I am.
My eggs keep running into hiding,
The coffee strives vainly to hiccup,
I leave a quarter for the singer,
a dollar for the poor.
Ask the women on the corner, how much for conversation?
They say they don't cater to perversions - try my luck next door.
I bump into an old friend who asks about my wife,
I say I didn't know I had one.
Then he's handing me a ten spot
says here go catch a cab.
I hand the driver a social security card
he says this ain't worth noting unless your old.
I tell him my hearts just gone arthritic
He says here pal try a gun.

Grandview Avenue

We were walking
Hand in hand
Up the hill
In the rain

You had your bright red scarf
Wrapped around your head
Traffic swished
Lights on
Wipers squelching

We didn't know what the day would bring
But I turned my face up to the sky
Trusting my own two feet and you to guide me

Morning Piece

This morning
Wrap myself
In a one of a kind memory
Close my eyes
Slip into my hands,
Cock my head back
Lean into a Manhattan Sunday
Just before summer
On the luxury side
Of uptown
Slightly smiling.

Jack, who no one reads

needing someone new to love
Loving/ needing newness
                            they loved
not understanding
no appreciating
not knowing
or caring
        he was it
                new
filling the need regardless of who he really was
something new
    a thing their parents never heard of
              would never approve of
                would at least be slightly threatened by
as if everyone would really go
     leave   pack it in
     give it up   hit the road

our highways then become our cities,
places like Manhattan our open roads?
     ~

But he brought you flowers
somehow knowing about irises.
sat down beside you
knowing about the gallery.
your being there
your thinking about your boyfriend.
your thinking about him in the dark room.
     ~

Turkish coffee at Mamoon's
afraid to wait any longer

that one time he was late
that day you were moving

from the city
from the summer
from all possibilities of being swayed

(for Gabrielle)

When I lived on West Main

When I lived on west main street
Third floor Victorian
Short walk for the liquor store past a little unnamed park
Not too far from downtown

Landlords' cousins on the first floor
Stole my unemployment checks
Put sugar in the gas tank
And I don't know why

We had a Great Dane, brindle dog
Got a cut on the end of his tail
And no matter what we did
He'd wag the bandage off.
Going up and down the stairs, hit the railings
Drops of blood splatter
As if his name was Jackson.

We bought a parrot
Called him Caesar
Filled the living room with plants
And let him fly around.

Got oil lamps to save on electricity.
Tall hurricane lamps,
Scented oil glowed in every room.
Tall well screened widows let the sky in.
Wood floors creaked waltzed all night by ghosts.

I went to work in a toy shop.
I was happy about the baby.
Still painted. Still wrote every day.
Still knew who we were.

It was the place where I'd smoke
As much as I wanted up into the middle of the night,
In that rocking chair your grandmother used to own.

Weight of endless summers in the dark.
Out over the roof tops, streaming lights, distant highways

Jenny

My fingers have touched
Your face
Your razor cut hair
Rose bud lips
Every square inch of how you define your
Slender secret self
Vulnerable to love
Shielded by the city
Defensive diaphragms
Nicotine & coffee
Shadow sister
Manhattan mono-chromed cool

Believing anything was possible we were the same

Beneath warm tones of old bones
Memories of girls and oceans
First born anxiety
Visitation eased by distance
Horizons met and thus reset
Soft steady ache like something summer upon green lawns
Time to talk in silence

Immortal Beloved

There is no such thing as Beethoven in Waterbury.
No one sees him buying race forms or cigarettes at Bauby's corner.
He doesn't play pin ball at Daz's,
chalk a cue at Gentlocks, pan handle a concert crowd at the
Palace theatre,
order Blue Ribbon shorts at Backstreet's or sit in Dresher's after
three sipping cool tall dark drafts.

He's not protesting the war at Library Park,
selling acid from the Kingsbury hotel,
falling asleep on Christmas eve with a girl named Mary in the
chapel of
St. Johns church.
Strung out girls don't get to build snowmen on the green with him
Mattatuck music can't hire him to move their stock
and the old man at Palace Liquors can't argue with him any-more.

Hare Krishna's can't get him to do their chanting.
Doorways where he stood out of the rain for hours are empty
or are gone.
Strangers at the all-night bus station, killers on
their way to Canada…
women from Louisiana… never meet him any-more.

He doesn't share a table with down-town Shirley and her father,
foretell the death of walking-stick Louie betrayed by Tiger Teddy,
sell more orange sunshine than Bobby Comfort,
blow a joint with the New Riders of the Purple Sage,
love a reincarnated baton twirling beauty queen from
North Carolina,
let catholic schoolgirls follow him home - cry
when he had to let them go.
He doesn't clamour along the roof tops with a friend named Bird,
who never got to California, find free warmth in the library or in
the stairwells of the Brown building or for a quarter a slice, get to
sit behind the pizza ovens at Dom-Nicks.
And no one sees him sitting on the fire escape drinking Roma
California Port with Whitey and Charlie Brown –
There's no such thing as Beethoven in Waterbury any-more.

On the corner of Lewis and West Main Beethoven's lover stands
Eyeing several schoolgirls waiting on a bench across the street.
There's nothing happens for her in this town any-more.
Yet still she dyes her hair red for him, refuses to ever ride a bus
And her pale lips still struggle with those Lucky Strikes
Just like always in his dreams

West Main Street

It rained the day you left
September ran like ribbons in the wind

I got a hold of some peanut butter and bread
Found a bag of pretzels in the living room
Sat on the front porch and fed

The streaks turned from red to puffs of broken white
The moon set on a sandy beach with the tide low
And there was only salt left in the bottom of the bag.

The City I Live in

stiletto fingers thorough search
organic testament
icy fluid release
bad colour rainbow
bread crumb numbs
in the aftermath
in the mean time
dry cruel patience
weight weight weight waiting
no exit
clung concrete tit
iron penis pierced
willing any piece for any price
for any sense of soothing

Morgana

I was awake, stars like angels
Spoke about you and me.
A golden moon so fine only by their whisper
Was it kept from disappearing?
Tiny drops of water leaned from every green thing
Yearning nourishment.

Your name deep measureless breath,
A hum of whales blue enough
So, every inch of everything could
Hear deep inside their minds, repeated.

Across high, seldom slack, storming,
Sightless of any land, oceans; I have written -
Have you lost more teeth?
What makes your tap-dancing men stay still?
Can immortality ever be mellow?
How other than stupor could it be done?

Answer-less.
As if the right combination
Could instigate response I keep trying new ones:
A girl with stones, started with daddy but now she's alone.
Names, dates, standard rates - charges extra for more.

Warm coffee streets,
Silence pressed around places we used to go,
Faces we used to know, now no longer clearly
Rather believed in, things thought and sometimes still
do think are true, even of ourselves

Dancing on the lake once covered Kathmandu valley
Sipping flowers fell from a sky beyond stars.
Smiling children marked by turquoise cobras
Great roots of great trees where
Grey matchless undisturbed as dust,
We'd rest.

The people who cured themselves

the people who had cured themselves
from the virus once called language
communicated eloquently
with their hands
with their arms
with their eyes
with the colour of their skin.

impossible to be misunderstood
they learned of the winds worship of leaves
the way the sun with every shadow enjoyed each day by day
and the height of midnight stars all sparkling –
happy with the moon, longing for its return.

eventually they forgot –
the coarseness of verbal abuse
the trickery of its seduction
the con of its half-truths.

made themselves dwellers on an island
rescuers, healers for those washed up from the deep
unafraid of reinfection they let the long-term healing of their lives
speak for them.

In the language of Flowers,
it meant we are already Dead

Beside whatever water there was
Overflowing tendrils
Draped swan songs
A capture of sorrow

reached out to nothing there
reached out to something ridged
Pulled from her heart
In and out
A pornograph of pain

A cruelty of cutlery
Memories picked clean
Ordinary such as all liquors are
A bed set with bones
Ignorant until that almost silly moment of surprise.

Every single question ever asked –
A useless pointless recycling

Somehow coming out at Robin's house
where she rescued us with coffee

That morning we walked into the snow
Across old farmlands
Over walls of field stone
The flakes large steady
Making it hard to see anything but them.
We'd stumble.
We'd fall.
Each of us
Quick to help the other.
Laugh sometimes,
Kiss sometimes.
Push ourselves forward.
Always forward.
semi shelter of thin woods,
 some nameless river,
   steepening ridge.
swirls of ever deepening ever dancing
mesmerised not bothering to melt snow
Clung
Like new eyelashes,
Like soft old useless flannel,
Like wishes from a childhood
Unable to be blown away
Or ever to come true.

This beach with my Mother

Tide comes Stronger now
Still myriad suns Roll upon the silver breakers

Day like the tide Has turned
Inevitable in its Priceless way

But for now, lingering A little longer
Simply sitting in the sun Breathing by the sea -
Not waiting for anyone

When I'm a ghost I'll haunt this beach with my mother

The little bay Where she'd sometimes stand
Looking out over the Atlantic, Imagining

I'd tell her it's OK
Anyone with that many kids Would imagine

I'd tell her Everyone's doing well
Everything pretty much worked out

Then we'd stand Look out over the sea
Imagining Forever.

As if the Rain

Emily Dickinson used to sneak out.
Sometimes in day light, mostly at night.
Tip toeing carefully down the back stairs
even though nobody else was there.
Always a hat a shawl or a veil
to keep the neighbours off her trail.
Walking along the streets of the town
glimpses her reflection among dry goods and gowns
and in the shop, she has been seeking makes her purchase
from a little man who has always honoured their agreement
and never her secrets has revealed.
Bag of tobacco, some skins and stick matches snapped into
her bag. While under her arm wrapped in brown paper
and knotted with string – a bottle of port.

Emily Dickinson used to sneak out.
Later that night she did it again.
Carefully tip toeing down the back stair
even though nobody else was there.
Making her way out to the train station,
counting the stars as she sat on the bench,
making up names for new constellations
while she was waiting.

An overcoat of stains and wrinkles
defines him as he sits beside her.
Sparkling eyes, familiar rodent hands
desperately tunnelling deep dead-end pockets
until rusty jack knife retrieved by one opened
by the other string and paper - slit and peel
turbulent mouth not spilling a drop
drained into a shudder of sighs
eases him back against the green slats.

things he knows he sometimes tells her:
crossing the country by freight.
tin can meals shared around a fire
men who only knew for certain that they'd not meet again.
bones broken by horses. bayonets emerging from a fog.
what it's like on the other side of the ocean.
names of young girls and young men.
who might be living? who might be dead?
and sometimes there's nothing to say,
only warm smoke shapes between them lingering
as if the rain would never come again
on a Tuesday night in Amherst...

Jackson Pollacked across
the empty linens of my bed

Your razors are my kisses
Your hands basin my heart
How often will you bleed me
And leave me in the dark?

I know how well you know me
I know you have no doubt
No matter what I try
No matter what I say
Can't change the way I feel
Don't want too anyway

My door is always open
So, you don't even need a key
got myself a new phone
no one but you has the number
So, no one else can bother me

Your razors are my kisses
Your hands basin my heart
How often will you bleed me?
And leave me in the dark

Nothing comes so softly as this day of leaving

even stones, once cursed
now picked up at random
savoured almost by mouth
a kiss let fall gently as if they'd remember only that
                no matter how much love we die
                no matter how much religion or philosophy
                eventually no one will remember us
                even history forgotten no matter what
                someday there will be no one left

as far as the eye can see small diamond stars tattooed
unspeakable skin
 ancient linens   a memory of water   a beautiful woman has come
pure infant dreams   deep on my strong shoulder   be good Tanya
be good
swaying songs, the rain peers into   I can see you twice in the mirror
walk into yourself
disappear

.

The Old Man I have sat with

anarchist veteran wars wound down across an age of cigarettes
jokes spun in and out upon the swirl of pastis and water
croissants and coffee through to charcuterie
against the warm summer stones of Montesquieu
old man and me, our laughter.
To not ever be forgotten,
our fear.

Decided to take the Highway

10 30   morning sun all out
everything steel and clear

traffic sparse
no road works
even the state police absent

I was heading north
I was hearing wolves
I was thinking about a girl I knew a hundred years ago
I hadn't anything to eat since yesterday
Sometimes I'd close my eyes

Last Poem before Oregon

Slept in groves of oranges
Visited by only wet nurse bees
Shaded by impossible leaves
Cloud drifting shapes of which made harlequin
Dreams disturbed gently by nimble hums
A voice like Marcello young again
Lip sticking fully curved
Remember the time
We discovered our deep lush alikeness
And rose, perfect stamens
A fruit of aching beauty
Wrote

(For Olga Blu')

Big Lorraine

I dreamed my love had found me
my children gathered too
put down all their weapons
eased their hearts cried their fill.
then they began to play
like they did when they were young
and when I woke, I'd forgotten
all my dreaming days were done.

I went down made the coffee
sat by an open window
ran my fingers through my hair
thought I heard somebody talking, voices carry on the air
birds out over the ocean rose silver like a prayer

Morgan

the Dogs Bay empty on a grey day
curves a wide scythe of sand
mimicked slopes of rocky hills dissolve again in low grey sky.

the Dogs Bay rings silver laughter a treasure of pearls
beautiful daughter darts like a needle between sea and sand
strangers, no choice, stop in their tracks, infected smiles.

not since the Indian Ocean where she learned to walk
not since Cape Cod where she learned her heritage
not since Cape Breton where she learned of treasure
has she now Connemara remembered

As Time goes by

days are always going on
streams of hours like cars trucks motorcycles
steadily scrambling through
as if on some desperate mission
important business somewhere else
not very often quiet
hardly any attention to my imagined rules of the road
I'm not important enough for a slowdown…
lucky the fuckers haven't come full stop I suppose.

Sitting on the back steps crying

In the language of flowers
It meant good-bye with regrets

Left on the kitchen table
An emptied cup of coffee
half-eaten slice of toast

Hardly a hesitation
Picks up the toast
Held away between thumb and finger
Some dead thing she didn't really want to touch

Steps out
Leans against the wood rail
As far as possible the offending slice
Tossed into the garden

As she does the wind
slams the door behind her
Startled but then relief,
Its off the latch…
As if somehow, he'd known…

The Magician's Hat

the woman in high heel boots
wishes she could pull out something
that would make her feel magical
something with a life of its own
something that might even bite her before
disappearing into an audience

but this hat only holds the emptiness of my heart
brim drooled by any rain drops
hemmed by smoke
softened by the oils of my head

realizing the age on my face
no explainable illusion
she does her own sleight of hand
dropping a thing once in her pocket
so, I can pretend to find it

The Oscar Peterson in my kitchen

The Oscar Peterson in my kitchen does not surprise me in my pyjamas.
I don't get to offer him a bowl of corn flakes while he's waiting
for my father.

No, the Oscar Peterson in my kitchen
has been dead for years and Dartmouth three thousand miles west
from where I sit.

Amazing October sun, solitude of coffee,
and when Billie chimes in
sure, isn't it just like heaven behind my eyes this morning?

(For jenny)

But our Love, not that kind

We had our own penises
taught them tricks -
sit up
roll over
play dead
beg

Had them fetch us things
Escort us on adventures
Put the seat up
Put the seat down
Not mess up the house

Whenever we wanted, we'd change them
Start again with new ones

Treats
Tricks
Travels
Toys

Sometimes they'd fall in love with us
 breaking their own little hearts

 But our love, not that kind,
Was only for each other.

Bigger than the Sky if a Star was your Eye

I have lived in houses of the dead.
Those who died before my age
Those who lived to be a hundred a hundred years ago.
Someday these stairs I sweep will still be here
And I will not be anywhere.
Someday all those I ever knew and who knew me,
No matter how intimately; will be no more.
Not even forgotten because there will be none
 Whoever even knew them or us or me.

My daughter age 7 asks "What happens when you die?"
"What really happens after you die?"

Am I afraid of death? Afraid of not being me anymore?
Am I afraid of life? Afraid of not knowing answers
Growing old? Forgetting?

My daughter loves the sea
we don't live near it, sometimes get to visit
dancing in and out the surf
Up and down the Dogs Bay regardless of the weather.

My son now in his thirties
hardly ever leaves his house
the one he bought from my father's estate
The house me and the siblings grew up in
Same ones I argued with, so he could live there
Like his grandpa said.

And maybe it's not so bad to forget?

Be free of history
be new
make space for right now
stop so much looking back.

And maybe it can be that way with death?
Not so bad, letting go of all this me?
Making space for something new?

But I've a strong ego, tuff as nails.
A Buddha's nightmare.
Veteran of all sorts of wars.
Maybe that's the equation:
stronger the ego – stronger the fear?

I am not the god of my children,
too old to fool them with immortality.
Anyway, they're too smart to not perceive my
purely human heart.

Love is not an answer but a response.
A response to all those unanswerable questions.

Not knowing anything, I love.
The more answers I don't have?
The more I feel my own true love.

So, I tell her –
I don't know what really happens when we die
But I do know how much I love you ~

The Avalon Girl

Met the darker double born.
Held her heart out to the heat.
Cut the braid from her own uncut head,
Gifted to his reckless wild hands.

Soon carried on to summery lands.
First crossed wastelands of the East.
Met a man who brought her peace.
Golden daughters dakini schooled.
Then rested into holidays & grandchildren,
Feasts begun to cook the night before,
Full house wakes up to a heaven scent.

And of her torn heart, spoke to none.
And of heat, preferred now a cooler Colorado sun.
And of her gifted young girl braid,
Remembered keen how the stupid jerk misplaced it.

But whenever she saw black upon the green.
Whenever 7 roses red appeared.
Whenever she saw the grey eyed sea.
No matter from which continent or shore –
Oh, she'd lose a heartbeat or two
And Avalon she'd think of you.

The Sea made her way

sneaking upriver
daring an overland short cut
crossed the lake
a hitched ride over the high land
 where the old man sat
back against white stucco
smoking a Cuban cigar

right away she began;
whispered
rolling waves
sounds of silver birds
stars like diamonds
pure black
as if travelling among them there
would never be another horizon

behind his eyes the old man smiled
o ribbons of smoke
barely audible ahh

at which she paused looked
saw him as he really was now
and knew all she could do was to return
from whence she came
never to kiss his pale grey eyes again

Mogambo

in the back yards of the moon
mountains ever silk with smoke
a cigarette a champagne
a dress for dinner
as if we would ever
be back
the only true things
ghosts unable to sleep
unable to abide this weight of age and flesh

princesses and big cats
a woman afraid of her own jungle
hunter of the caged
a man afraid of mortality
how could our hungers meet?
How could our true nature reveal?
those ghosts we fear so much
are all the spirit we could have been.
All we traded away so cheap.

In the obligations of our evenings
in the entitlement of our heritage
sweat black the spear singers
sweat black the towel holders
as if the pale god held sway
without the guns of our own steel,
without the cripple nature of our own fears
we could never make our way a way

Windowpane

The night has its own creatures
Familiars like foxes, bats,
Owls, green eye cats
And others more unique,
Those without a daytime shape
Shifting shadow colour forms
Billow through dissolving walls
Entwine upon my outstretched arms
Feed on darkness through the night
Until there's nothing left but light

Snuggle

Snuggle, snuggle
Little girl
In your nice warm bed
Snuggle snuggle
Little one
Lay down, lay down you sleepy head
Dream away till morning.
Princess with two-star tattoos
On her cheek n forehead

The fairies loved this story
How she came to stop the roaring
~
Wake up wake up
My little one
We have a busy morning

(For morgan macha)

For the ice to heal

From the kitchen window
Curtain less

Stiff abandoned on the line
Since October, Sentinel dish towel
Clumsy signal, Waves

Not yet
Not yet

Might as well
Another coffee

Something for the birds
Rare as rubies cardinal
Blue jay bright stuns my eyes
Dull small brown little things

Ok
Ok
First thing tomorrow
Auger from the garage
Break that agreement Made with myself
To wait

Three Greys

On the floor
Looking up
skylight
Edges of blue
shape into disappeared.
   Where the world ends
    Does sky begin?

Faucet chromed
Pitted bright 'n dark
Bumpy capitol C
Marks an asterisk tap
Turned
Brown sputter brown
Pop pop popping
Into clear n smooth

Soft morning
Bird song people
I cannot see walk
Hearing their voices
Dogs bark

Fuckin' Bukowski

Idiot me picks now
6000 miles away at 52
To *discover* him
Still glad I didn't stay in Waterbury
Find him sooner
Probably still be pukeing
Out in the after last call
Parking lot of now what am I gonna do
Or else back in jail
Or else still with one of the xes
Or else not even alive
~
Tonight, just had a chicken and ham sandwich on rye
And its sometime after midnight
And I'll probably still be up @ 6 maybe half 6
Do some yoga make coffee for the wife
Bring it to her in bed
Get some pancakes going for the kid
And be happy to do so
~
No not envious
Not regretful
Rather peaceful
Glad to be out of it
That's the kind of poet I'm happy to live with Now.

Because of Patrick

Would I were on raglan road
When days and nights still soft like raindrops fell.
Unnoticed smokes occasioned by good porter
And I wanderer of no particular destination
Knew by heart each foot fall path I'd take
To find myself back home again

Ex's - a word poem

Surplus
Glut
Overload
Surfeit

Shortage (Antonym!!)

Overindulgence
Intemperance
Immoderation
Dissipation

Moderation (Antonym!!!)

Extra
Additional
Surplus
Spare
Leftover

Previous
Past
Earlier

Open Heart Surgery

Time has passed
And aren't we old and settled in our ways?
Funny with all our differences
How similar we have become.

But still I don't know what to do around you
Magnificent stranger, significant giant.
If you were my mother laying there, we'd hold each other
Maybe cry together

And wouldn't I love to?
But isn't it scary?

So, in true manly fashion
I lay the blame on you
Without saying a word
Better safe and sore –

Isn't that the man thing?
Love the wound.
Fear the healing.

Love Poem for R.B.

Today I heard on the radio that Richard Brautigan
Killed himself last fall.
Then some girl who was 17 in 1970 read his Love Poem.
She said that her then lover was a DJ on a college
Station and had dedicated a recording of the poem
To her, over the air, before he disappeared in a
Californian direction.

Anyway, I don't know where I was.
Maybe I was washing clothes or asleep even,
Or maybe I was with Jenny or Eva or somebody.
I could a been drunk or depressed
As if by some sort of intuition;
All I really know is that I'll never know where I was
When he did it.

I wonder how he did it.
Maybe I should go down to the library look him
Up on the newspaper micro-film file?
Most likely I won't though, the library is closed now
And I'm not sure I care that much anyway.
Besides it's one of those details I'm sure will
Accidentally find its way to me.

It kinda pisses me off that he did it, I mean he
Wrote that Watermelon Sugar book, I read it
When Mary gave it to me and me, 15 in 1970.
Watermelon Sugar and Mary my first lover go good together;
But I don't know about this suicide stuff.

But maybe
It's nice
Not having to wake up alone with yourself
When you just don't want to anymore.

(6/6/85)

Tom Ruff

pedal steel
rain greying reflection
Kerry fishermen pulling nets
framed now by geraniums as well
she walked over to the window
"Looks like the sky's on fire." she said.
"Maybe it is." he said, still half buried in the duvet.

The Star your brother sent for Christmas

I still have the star your brother sent for Christmas
When you were far from home here in America.
Gold foil folded origami-like, eight points.
you were a little bit crying.
it meant so much to you.
I keep it;
in a book, big enough to protect it, Picasso Lithographs,
safe just the way you'd remember.

Poetry from the Edge

maybe if I stayed
paid my dues
drunken disorder
hometown wives
possession with intent
liberal arts and all that shit
reading at the button wood tree
slams at the museum
out for macrobiotic afterwards with students and faculty
but I didn't

instead
carrying with me every step of the way
bones broke by horses
planes to airports languages I couldn't say
waited all day for you in the grand canary
rode alone desert near Giza
stranded in Aswan after ships curfew
walking frozen January rivers in Hamburg
drove 14 hours straight as far as I could go to end up in Ohio
waited hours at Mamoon's for someone named for angels
never showed
stood alone on street corners 3am waiting on a bag of coke

hope you're doing well
having a wonderful time
glad I'm still here.

American Boots

ready to ride into the sunset
just like all the dreams raised up by our fathers
we could always go, just leave
honourable self-exile
to the wars, to the west, to the open oceans,
wagon trail highways silver mines lodge pole pines

places you need to know how to gut a deer
catch bare handed fish
start fires without matches
navigate by stars
use a knife to heal yourself
figure out the safety of water before you drink

find comfort in doorways
locked boarded up homesteads
lean-to stones
bare branch trees
even in winter even in pitch black nights
even when all you ever thought you knew was only
something left behind

Wordsilk

reminding me of words like
border line
crescent coyote
ancient timbers
polished smooth as kisses
paradise
abandoned eyes of shipwrecked sailors
myriad of pin prick suns
flightless birds
something Spanish that you said along a twilight turquoise
Ishmael to Ishmael
all the nights we've ever known
not bothering the quiet.

Come down from your hills

Come down from your hills and see me
Remind me when I was a girl
Tip my kisses with honey
Bathe my feet in your curls

Soft green grass in showers of gold
Apple blossoms swirl like snow
Echoless laughter my hands on your face

Come down from your hills and see me
Remind me when I was a girl
I'm tired of long wool skirts
Tired of wobbly shoes
Tired of being a stranger afraid to remember you

That's why

Lived the life
Walked the streets
Did the drugs
Drank the booze
Had the lovers
Bled the blood
Took the wounds
Allowed the scars
Starved froze
Waited pleaded fought screamed whimpered
Abandoned forced schemed -
Learned all these leave the muse unmoved.

But I could tell you, if you would hear
How it was when blessed by her
How it felt – all golden honey all hyper hungry a buzz
of multiplicity a cellular splendour of free flight
No pen pencil typewriter computer recorder nothing -
able to keep up
All I have ever written a pale reminiscence

So yeah why would I care if anyone reads?
Well because someday I'll get it
Express that inexpressible
With words that when read it can be got.
That's why!
That's why!
And when I do, then you'll wish
You'd been following all along.
free from the shackles of words, the tyranny of
language

Not quite Tomas

crosses the church yard
with a woman that would have been Sorcha if it were

how much more than footsteps
between us now

yet still I look
expecting him has caught my eye

there used to be horses before Cabra
sanctuary on the Liffey

our children would meet, play,
remember one another's birthdays

The Tree the Wind lives in

the tree the wind lives in drowses
a whisper something on the road
rain windows your passing soul
promises like rides to every hitchhiker never kept
smoky speculations headlight hide and seek
upon some kind of lace hung by my visiting mother
as if ever earned a simple gratitude

P.F.C.

crossing the country by train
deep water port
shore of dreams
golden gateway rising sun
grey steel ships
grey steel sea
grey soft eyes

fraternity of fear and obligation
naivete and boredom
a steady bravado
a tedium of active duty

battered, dog-eared but never
a note not even your name in,
Shakespeare, bible of complete works hidden away
secret claim to dreams your heart could not reveal

Sitting

A man's hands on a girl's thighs
  One on each roll them out
  A better view of what he's dreamt for so long.
  Muscular even in yielding
  She allows her deep breath body freely.

Outside women talk how the year slips
School days into holidays beginning school again

A woman in love writes her name
  Moon soft ivory
  Pale sky
  By the Buddha
  By the open window
  Major piano chords
  A simple charm
  Like where in dreams we can't be hurt.

 A man begrudging poetry
  Leaves out such things as joy
  Hopes a mirage of his own making
  Hides in clothes made from mistaken identities
  Secrets like superman behind caped crusades
  Although blurred some character always lurks
  Despite the roles he thinks he should,
  He thinks they want; he thinks he must.
  A series of figures exchanged throughout his life
  Even the god he picks a model of dysfunction.

Do Do Run Run

after the show she'd call him
wait with the security guys out back
in the open doorway if it was raining
watching waiting smoking.
she'd heard they added menthol to 'em so you
wouldn't feel what they were doin' to your throat,
she wasn't sure about that – maybe there's just too much mistrust
in the world.

anyway, it never took him long,
no matter what the time was
even if the show ran late
even if there was snow
she never had long to wait.

Hop out the car run up them iron stairs
and she not really smiling not even when, every time
he'd kiss her before saying hello and how was the show?
walk her arm 'n arm to the car,
open and close her door.

she was back up singer in a steady small-town gig.
the one who wore a black beret
sang better 'n most of the leads she broke her ass to make look good.
and maybe if she were younger…
and maybe if she weighed a little less…?

back home,
he'd always have something good and warm and ready to eat
and sometimes in the shower the hot water lasts an hour
and sometimes she'd have a little something strong to drink.
and he'd put something on the stereo real low like madam butterfly
and lay her down until falling asleep
only by some taunting dream she'd wake
to find his arms still around her.

Minor Miracles of the Sea

They would meet in passing
Eventually she would when they were speaking ask,
Why was he here in the dead of winter?
Winter was not dead, he said, but it was clean.
And together they agreed.
There was no one else.

Sometimes they would discover things together
An eroded seal carcass, tubular ribs of something else unknown
A drifting buoy setting out to sea – free at last

Sometimes snow came
And they knew each other only by the shape of their footprints
Criss crossing unsynchronised in time but not in space

Once they came together at the little inlet
Waves frozen mid act now in gentle breeze like chimes
a music she had never heard before
And neither he said have I.

Twilight Zone Episode Love Story

That afternoon she came into the bar
told me she had something to tell me
could I please come outside?
Please.
Sure, I said.
It was a light spring day, maybe even summer
we stood together on the little concrete steps
front door of the bar.
I was probably leaning against the railing
most definitely smoking.
She stepped down to the sidewalk
looking up she said
listen, I just have to tell you…
some other guy she met; really thought he was the one.

I'm so sorry she said.
I offered to buy her a drink – for old times'
No, she said.
I'm sorry I made you sad
I'm sure you'll find someone too.
Goodbye
she paused,
thanks for being so understanding.
You really are a good man you know.
And left.

I went back in. Joined Scutter at the bar. Lit a smoke.
Ordered us a round.
In those days we were drinking gin on the rocks with a
splash of rose's,
we were smoking Philip Morris like the attorney
general was loony tunes,
we were betting on the NFL like it owed us a paycheck.

Anyway, before she came by,
I had been telling him how I was in a bit of a jam
with this young girl
she was so into me, didn't have the guts to break her heart.

Jesus, he said after I told him she'd just dumped me,
That was like some twilight zone episode love story.

Foggy Misty Morning

birds sing longer dawn gone slower
soft diffused glow
tempted to stay in bed
not wanting to miss one moment
push myself to rise instead

golden Buddha
sky blue sky
prayers carried by wind
white & blue green & red
blown beyond belief

Whose name began with Stars

the man whose name began with stars
combed like golden curl searched silence

went through forests withheld blame
through deserts called out names unlike his own

took shots with chances so long no one ever knew where they
landed
cried into nights so long it terrified god

expected nothing got more than he bargained for

and when the time came for secrets whispered to his long dead
mother
remembered midnight hair, red red lips, eyes the colour of
someplace else

cool skin, pale airless, hello goodbye kisses,
deep as if oceanic swells her voice

Continuum

they meet full force frontal
as if the harder they fall the deeper they'd go

but the amount of space between them?
same as any other, a whole universe'd fit into it.

Smoky Pelican

I have known there
those eyes like Canada
mostly dark vacant cold
wake with sudden flashes
no slumber impenetrable
a last boat before the ice
chugs like some crazy kids skipping rope
missing a beat beat   beat
before returning reassuringly to proper rhythm

time to go
minutes as if fast food
wrapped in Styrofoam
tucked in a rolled-up bag
held one handed
push the door
out into the world quick
as if what was lost could ever be something to be found

Anymore of days

I don't much keep track anymore of days
soft grey eyes passing opportunities
a train crossing the country
stones in a warm corner of sun
something else I was supposed to do forgotten.

The Disappeared

Along the lane
Straight down as rain
Without wind
Without sound
Wrapped in briar vines
Emerging posts of bone
As if some ancient mariner
Draws me in
Secret un-loved caress.
I wanted to keep you
For myself.
I wanted you to stay,
Because you went.
But the police,
After further questioning
Came up with ideas all their own
And in so doing, made contact with
The families of the disappeared.

Occasionally
To men in long wrinkled coats, they speak,
A fog of voices drifting apart,
Before reaching any type of destination.
Taking turns, they cast their looks around,
As if this really were sea
And answers like shoals of silver fishes lurk
Just beneath the surface.
While careful to pretend not to notice
How each movement flickers in the lights

As if this really were 1922 and all some cinematic image
Screened with no one but the actors in the audience.
Their own silences magnifying certain sounds:
Elastic latex snap,
Slicing shovel slaps,
Unsteady cigarette sighs,
Plastic, almost echo, abruptly ending, long metallic zip.

Believing their expectations to be accurate predictions
They came for something clear and full of meaning,
Something settling and complete,
To find, as if some great surprise,
Only the obvious inescapably revealed.
Unlike them I know you not by what you lost,
But rather by what you have brought back.
It was that which drew me
In secret un-gloved caress
And now plays out
Along the landscapes of my every night
And haunts my every morning with regret.

I wanted to touch that forbidden you again.
To trace upon that more secret map
Etched, invisible to the naked eye,
Every line of your journey.
To put my lips to you,
Circling with the tip of my tongue,
So that I'd know, everything.

Litchfield

Used to walk by trees like these, even in winter when black like
the stone walls beside them. It was a time between horses, I was
alone except for a couple of friends who took me in, not so far
from where I used to live. When I was still married. The wife and
I, we'd ride these old dirt roads of New England. Thick second
growth woodlands occasional colonial ruins, old fields skeletal
marked, ubiquitous stone walls in the middle of everywhere
and nowhere. On the open stretches sometimes, we'd race. She
always won. Even when we'd swap horses; she always won.

So eventually alone along this tree lined ridge, straight old dirt
road closed to modern traffic, walking that perfect strip to race.
Hoping since it was now deep winter, she'd stay home not ride
by me or if she did, she'd not recognize me - or that if she did
come by she'd stop, not go on ignoring me? But it was cold deep
winter, and I knew she didn't much like it. She might be sat by
the fire, possibly in town. More likely down the islands where it
was plenty warm, people knew her there.

Made my way to some place I knew existed, crook of a stone wall
slight shelter from the gale to flick, fumble , eventually light a
sacramental cigarette - to the east, to the south, to the west, to the
north, as above so below, as within, so without, on this smoke
that is my prayer...
For this snow, this wind, this gunmetal sky,
this cold, cold, cold against the small heat of my beating heart...
Thank you

First Kiss

I remember the music
When you were 16
Pretending to dance
So, I could feel you close
Whenever I did, you'd laugh

It was slow 2, 3, slow 2, 3,
 We swayed we leaned
Found out what we smelled like behind each other's ears
But we didn't care much because we didn't let go.
    Your hands all polished white, fingers stronger than any
                                        small thing

I remember the music
When you were 16
Soft sweet
A slow mystery

Moving together
Surprised by ourselves
 Moonless summer night
Even in shadow closed our eyes,
 Bumped our noses …

 I remember the music,
   But lately can't seem to picture your face
     That's how it is these days,
Memories unhurried slip
 Like horses,
     To other greener places, sometimes though returning
                                    on their own…

Hands

even now when all I have of your memories
stirred up by photos in a Sunday magazine
someone I never heard of
someone not resembling you at all

except for hands

blue lines, brown skin, pushed by invisible muscle
all summer and horses and hot salty workdays
so much sweeter when tipped by my tongue
saddle soaping rip cord fingers
guiding me to wherever it was I'd need to go

La la La la la

I am rolling on the waves
on the waves
on the waves
I am rolling on the waves
far away from shore

The sun is shining not too strong
not too strong
not too strong
The sun is shining not too strong
far away from shore

Happy dolphins guiding me
guiding me
guiding me
Happy dolphins guiding me
far away from shore

The Buddha trees

I have escaped.
Finding myself
In a foreign country
Smoking endlessly free tobacco
Finding myself
Only able to sit by this window
Looking at trees
One after the other

I have escaped.
Finding myself
In new running shoes
Safe among strangers
Finding myself
Only able to hear music in my head
La la la la la   la laaa
A woman's voice
As if asking,
Could I take up my instrument once more?
As if saying,
Together we could skip through spring once more
As if trusting the concealment of trees had been enough

Flora's Yard

A September still day
cricket sounds
rippling sunlight.
soft breeze
cool dream echoing
with memories and moonlight.

There in maple shade
her potted plants,
having sucked up morning
their greedy leaves
strain, now for afternoon.

Christmas

heavy dark seeded bread
brown bottled beer you can't see through
dry sharp salami
lumps of malachite shaped into eggs
glass beads ready for stringing
sheets of tin
strands of copper
steamy dark tobacco wrapped with yellow papers
messages from gypsy horsemen distant relative to our mother

How you look today

you ask for
softer clothes
something
complimentary
to nudity
you remember
types of
warm
lips
firm fingers
drapesing rhapsody
you think of time
patiently
savouring lozengy
past loves
live moments
even regret
luxurious
soon wrapping
silk confidence
check mate your way out
silver day bright
sheer white
high altitude blue
a waiting

Learning to be Friends with the Rain

~

if I put each of these days
end to end
how many times around the world
would they go?

~

no matter what
yes
the only choice

~

living in the peace
so many would die for
I walk the dogs
 old growth
cross clear brooks
splash for drinks

~~~~~~~~~~~~~~~~~~~~~~~~~~~~~~~~~~~~

sometimes this sense of failure
is all I'll ever be
sometimes that loneliness
is all I'll ever see

~

it's the price for being true
it's the cost of no surrender
the double helixed blessing
of being me

~

maybe tomorrow
the courage will come
all that ever was –
undone

Draped in white

went down by the house you used to live in
all the windows had the same curtains
the one where your bedroom was, open
for a moment
draped in white
your invisible hands
wave
~

Loretta's Piece
(12.09.73.)

Rose was first thought
remembering was coming
but put back almost worn out.
Now – when roses bloom
not trying for anything.
Now when I am and am not
then or pretty soon.
Now when words burn meaningless
giving warmth
to bodies
already left behind
the thoughts are all,
growing weeds
coiling snakes
blooming
gaping
the flesh we cared for
the planet we cared for
the stars we strived for.

Looking at our World

if we truly see the world as it is our hearts would break.
and if our hard and well protected hearts broke
then they would become truly soft.
what if we all treated the world with softness,
the natural softness of a human heart?
is that buddha
is that Christ,
is that the Goddess
is that Allah,
God, Krishna
Zeus?
I don't know but it could be us
and if were us, what would it look like then?

Mara

always willing to go
always yes, never no
protector of my daughter
her first-time home alone
days so grey I couldn't imagine telling anyone else about –
you were my only confidante
where you are now
I don't know
but there' s this place in my heart
where, whenever I call,
I know you'll come
do dogwoods grow in this country?
if so, this spring I'll plant one where you lie

The Poet

Never did the ride she really wanted, tack that chestnut mare,
Out before daybreak. Just the two of them.
Saddle bags packed. Enough to get started.
No plans for coming back.

Now a cross between memory and fantasy, a someday kinda
thing -

How many years has someday now become?

Haven't we all touched the world with little fingers,
Seen the world through tears,
Breathed the air breathed by everybody else.
Once our hands were small enough to be held by another,
Once we saw the world as full of wonder.

Alone is a place where anything can happen,
No matter where it's always there,
Dark like streets you're not afraid of,
Deeper than sky reflections on an unknown lake,
A sunset trail,
Stars you can walk off into

Billy the Kid in Hamburg

Billy the kid in Hamburg
On the run from what he didn't know
Brought his six guns, slid down his hat,
Night robbing trains by lantern light.

Secreted señorita homesick for palm trees & tequila
Small stories of her Badlands youth
Explains to him the length of her long legs
And how she knew she'd never have his kids.

Down in the Reeperbahn, softly smoking
Cigarettes he didn't know how to roll, so she did.
As if hot grog and sailors
Could detour him from
Whatever treasures he'd go back for.

And she'd hear how he'd gone for some golden princess
steeple swayed,
Belief in orthodoxy still strong especially when so
far away from home
Until eventually surrounded by things even he couldn't deny,
Wrapped his pistols in dirty laundry packed in a trunk,
Trusted to the stations of trains, fortune of strange ports,

Back in the land where he was born.
Severely betrayed, nearly captured on the river
Escaped by some woman so strong she scared him
But from whom he learned to ride -
Life of horses,
Long constantly moving horizons,
Real living breathing freedom between his legs.

And whoever couldn't understand his guns
Abide the smell of horses
Take those chances freely offered,
Wouldn't they still love him?
Lead him into parlours, boudoirs,
Soft green grassy banks secluded by whatever river –
Until once more his own true nature breaks their law?

Where her breasts used to be

kissed her courage
her fear
her sadness
her deep unknowability
because she was dearest
because she was all love
and all love would ever wish to be

Waltzing Miss Jeanie

The sky barely visible
Gunmetal cold keeps each bit of snow completely separate.
Sounds, most into silence or muffled by a swish and swirl
As my horse moves through.
Imagine sand against a giant hourglass,
Wicked witch of the west,
There's no place like home…

Nothing else moves,
Rock walls mostly covered
Drain ditches camouflaged
Snow drifts level the landscape beyond illusion.
By memory only we keep to the road.
Imagine being the first to cross this land in winter
And if it were a time before horses…?

Off the open ridge we cut down to where the pine woods
Shelter enough so we can pick up the pace.
Occasionally overburdened snow spills,
Sometimes peeling bits of green, chunks of old ice, thuds magnified
by the quiet.
Perhaps an excuse to break monotony
Or some primal memory aroused –
She spooks.
Imagine double barrel blast, a restless dragon, a living legend…

So, I talk her through; my voice being a calm place for her to focus.
So, I sing, putting the name she knows into the song,
My fathers' curious choice for a lullaby he used to sing to me.
Imagine not yet five years old, frightened from things that you don't
even have words for.
Things that move only in those darker places in your room,

And then his heavy footsteps, the weight of his body as he sits on the edge the bed, his strong steady hands sometimes rubbing sometimes patting while always singing over and over until finally asleep you couldn't ask him to again…

We make our way like that now,
Dealing with imagined as well as real risks –
Patches of ice beneath this rising snow upon this rising, winding road

The Girl

Call her flower by moonlight
Cypress by spring
Watch from the evening
Change to grey misty morning
Leaving the Stars Behind
Across the spider down day

How long my unfitting skin, the night

she had come down from Gunnison
it had been a hard ride
thin air refusing to support her
old shoes needing to be thrown away as soon as possible
~
met over drinks at The Last Chance
 told me brief stories
life in the wilderness
ways of ghosts and proud flesh
we booked a room from the man who wore a star
~
make believe log cabin
steel spring mattress
Jim Beam on the bed side
we smoked silent shapes into an invisible ceiling
I was happy to be there
 she was too
~
but somewhere after moon light
she had gotten up
kneeling by the drifty window
to whatever she prayed
all I could make out was –

How long my own unfitting skin the night?

What is the Ordinary?

a leaf
a blade of grass
ground we walk on
air we breathe

blue sky
black sky
stars drift
moon shifts
sunset
 sunrise
what is the ordinary?

tide water
still water
flower bloom
insect buzz
bird song on the wing
what is the ordinary?
your birth
your self
your child
your lover
your life
your death
what is the ordinary?
explain it to me please

The Orphan as Adult

my eyes were not green for you
I did not rebel or lead
never even learned to read.
children dropped from me
in a pain no one cared about.
my years marked by long days and short lives.
as if expecting greeting, you return.
as if your photographs meant something
other than a young girl momentarily annoyed
her world same now as it was then
a place where things just are the way they are.
my eyes were not green for you
only an accident of birth
same as your own.

These Words

from the tiredness of my bones
not syllables of warm water mouths
rather emanate rich with marrow silent sensations
hot cold
soft foetal
crescents of your ears
depth deeper than you know of your eyes
the vast rift of tears
your endless heart
alone sometimes in the dark
I have been a labour for you
silently aloud
likewise you should read
these words so unlike other words
each window through which invisible creatures
of what cannot be said climb

Not the Pretty One

We were not the pretty ones
Everyone we loved
Would never care for us
The way we'd want them to

Being achievers
We achieved
A toleration
Sometimes an invitation

But we were not the pretty ones
No matter what
We couldn't achieve that

So, one day it struck me
Stunning logic obvious
And the next time I saw you I asked
And when you answered
I got it, I understood
It was never a we thing

Nocturnes at the Borders

a long passing caravan of days
deserted debris
   hope a pitch-black oasis –
sparkling the only un-still things
such as stars, jewel throat ghosts,
your eyes beyond all knowledge,
the only dark that shines –
   a different kind of sun.

my mouth for your love
dreams smoke wandering horizons
red glow desert
a voice wet silk
drawn as if my skin
found out in the wind
perfumed by foreign creatures
nourished by such exploring
my heart contains a fertile seed
   A treasure trove for beetles an insect paradise.

I saw you with tears in American gowns
you were just like Picasso but knelt on the ground
as if genuflecting before the print page you'd inhale
the spirit right out of his grave and I just couldn't
take it so I wandered around as if I could shake you
Like salt from my skull
   Always returning an orbit of doubt.

The scent of your soapy skin draws me in
ways I cannot identify

like ivory in the morning someplace else away
beyond a snow tipped mountain
before the savannahs open prayer
dark meandering luxurious survival
Our daring selves mortal among the Edens.

With Jesus in Jacksonville

Went out rolling n hitting the bars
Bumped into each other got sacramental
After last call
Wished hard for a car without a locked door.

In a blue & white Bel Air
Fixed on a higher power
Rolled up a Jerusalem
Floored it

Stopped out on some twisted ridge
Wandered So far away
When the cops finally showed
We didn't even have to run.

And we wished for something we could do.
Something to keep things at bay.
Some way to swear all that we done
Would still be so in the light of day

On my Mother's side

My mother never told me
The one thing I'd 'a listened to most.
Diagnosed with cancer (7 years before it killed her.)
Deciding to keep it to herself,
She did exactly what it wanted -
Believing it was for her children's benefit, how would she refuse?

Besides my mother came from a family of secrets
Dark Sicilian secrets emanated from
Every Sunday dinner table that ever was
Ebb   Flow   Echo   Repeat
Dance through generations none of us immune

free from all the ancient stories I
could have held the woman who gave me birth
cried any tears together
faced fear until it became compassion
looked into her eyes knowing it was goodbye
and that there would never be another word between us

Siane

1.

He truly loved the land more than anyone ever did,
As if this loving could make the land forget
how he had come, as one adopted through the wedding chamber.
With scepticism and disdain the land responded,
for this sentimental tender love - this was not enough!
And the horses? Well they adored him.
Their noses quivered at his presence,
 they raced, stood up on their hind legs, sang for him
 even took bites out of each other to draw his attention.
But they would not let him ride.
For they were brothers and sisters with him.
 Beloved companion, never to be considered master.
  And he? He admired the land for its strength, how it
showed to him
its true face. For that he said "What great spirit, a terrible beauty.
How fortunate I am to be chosen to see the true face of the land."
  Towards the horses he was also grateful and for that he said
"What noble blood, what rare beauty. I am so fortunate to be
allowed to know their secrets."
  While the land and the horses both looked to one another and
said, "Well what can you do with a man like that?"
  Now she, who had taken the man to her wedding bed,
she held the land tight with her own hands and so marked it with
her own blood. That was how the land was won. Her own flesh
protecting, defending and willing to do so over and over - That
was how the land was kept.
  It was she who led the horses to shelter when the sky burst at
midnight. Kept them from prairie fires, dipped her hands into
their mothers at the time of their birth and with a voice of smooth
leather and singing bees subdued even the boldest among them.
  To the land she was forgiving. Admiring its resilience, she
would say "So beautiful yet so obstinate - you are the breaker of
my heart, but I will never leave you."

To the horses she was wise and often amused would say "You make me laugh when you try your tricks on me, but I won't let you forget our bargain."

While the land and the horses long ago had looked to one another and said, "Well what can you do with a woman like that?"

The man of course could not understand all the ways of his wife. In his opinion her discipline kept her from appreciating the beauty that surrounded her. But he would also say, as was his nature, "I admire her strength and abilities. Truly this is a magnificent woman. If she were not my wife and therefore part of me, I should envy her these things."

The woman at first was quite perplexed regarding her husband. She suspected perhaps some flaw in a man who would refuse to master things in a way similar to her own. On this she pondered for some time before concluding that because of his way, surely, he had never known loneliness. So, then she did say, "My husband has this nature which I cannot myself afford to indulge in. Yet it is also true that being joined to me he can do this for us, and we will both benefit from the balance."

So, their wisdom of what a marriage truly is prevailed and luckily so for me because that is what I was born into.

My parents of course taught me their ways.

With the horses my mother taught me how to ride,

My father, how to share their secrets.

She, how to hold the land.

He, that I could love it more than anyone who ever saw it.

And I, being a true issue of their wedding bed,

Understood both and formed a way of blending each, a way of my own.

2.

When I was born, I saw the world through the eyes of a crow. For at least three maybe four days. On the day the crow returned my soul to my body I was able to see through my own eyes. The first person I saw through such eyes was she who was my nurse. When I was older, she told me of this event. Explained how I was special because usually crows do not return such a lost or stolen soul. How children's souls are so sweet they are usually eaten right away. But she had this feeling about me and stayed by me constantly during those days so that my worried parents might try to get some rest. I asked her if it was because my soul was not sweet that it wasn't eaten? She laughed and told me that even the most wicked person was born with a sweet soul.

So, what did I see when I saw through the eyes of a crow? Well one day as I was still child enough that all chairs were big enough for me to curl up in, I did so in the kitchen. Staring into the fire I heard the voice of my nurse, softly, tenderly she spoke and quietly falling asleep still hearing her voice I began to dream. and she, from whom I have never had reason to doubt and from whom I have only known loyalty and love, this is what she says I told her from my dream state about the times when I saw through the eyes of a crow:

A great grey sky almost to rain. leaves gone to colour muted by soft and steamy morning. While Below, arched like great green cat backs, farming lands bordered by trees rowed up like man soldiers behind walls of stone which long ago toilers of these fields had so piled. Then as if in memory I saw them, those man-things building walls. Stones like teeth, roots like tendons pulled from a dark open earth. Then as if in further memory I saw those same lands in a time before the man-things, a time when all was tall forest, hard wise wood forests before the man-things came....

But now its only overgrowth, sapling and briar borders along these scrubby pastures where I must keep my attention. Now my vision follows the lay of the land, rolling down to a small valley curling with a silver stream then over again until directly below me a field just before the water slips into the woods. A field now for the dead of men. Vivid in an otherwise dull landscape their blood pulls at me. A rare moment - Not only much flesh but are none among them upright, none to bury these fallen in the ground as if some seed to sprout anew. Now they are still, delicate, exposed, but I cannot let my vision linger long. There are my comrades feeding, they will leave aside some favourite scraps for me. But I cannot let my vision linger long. I the watch must keep... Until, on a young and therefore tender one, my comrades call "Come. Come. Come." with a will of their own my legs push off. The earth happy to see me rushes up in greeting and with a jolt I'm standing wide awake before the kitchen fire.

3.

Real magic has the quality of knowing. By paying attention you get to know things and when they will happen. With this knowledge you can create the illusion that you cause the inevitable to happen. Real power is when you have people convinced that they can't get along without you. But there are other things, things beyond people. Once I convinced the wind that it couldn't get along without me.

I'd go out to the top field where the horses ran free. Where they worried themselves with petty

grievances grazed as they wished regardless of day or night and sometimes lay like dead things strewn - lulled by whatever dreams it is that horses dream. On a grey garneted out crop of lichened stone I stood, turned my face to the sky and this is what I said:

"If I could be anything in the world
I would be the wind.
To kiss the sea.
Embrace the sky
Caress the earth.
Come wind I call you
Bring the rain, bring the storm,
The lightning and the thunders roar.
Come wind I love you!"

I tried this several times and sometimes the wind would come
up strong while others calm and quiet. In other words, I made no
impact whatsoever.   But I did not give up. By now the horses took
notice of my antics and drew around as if seeking inspiration from
my sermon on the mount. Perhaps they found some, but the wind
did not. Once I got so angry this is what I said:

> "If I could be anything in the world
> It would never be the wind,
> insignificant bastard of the heavens
> Ignorant victim of a manipulative earth,
> carrier of piss   spittle   bird droppings
> owner of dust and ashes...."

At this did the wind hesitate for a moment before it went back to
ignoring me? No. Eventually the horses too lost interest in my
daily ritual. After all I brought no carrot or apple, didn't respond to
their sparring for attention, was as bored as they with those rearing,
bucking, bluffs.

 Finally, I decided to give up. I decided that if I couldn't be master
then I would surrender. So, I said when the wind was quiet,

> "As the wind is quiet and still, so am I."

And too if the wind moved from the East I would say,

> "As the wind I too move from the east."

So, it was with every direction and with every temperament. As
gentle breeze or herald of the storm and too through the seasons
such as that of summers comfort or raging winter's howl. For a
whole year this was my daily practise. There were times when
I thought I'd be carried away, dragged along the ground or else
motionless so long I 'd drop from fatigue but this did not happen.
I began to know the wind, a scent on the air, look of the sky,
temperature from yesterday compared with today, slight almost
invisible trembling dry leaves - all were signs. So closely did I
follow that I became as a shadow to the wind.
In time my movements became just slightly ahead until it was I
who cast a shadow called the wind.

Once more in late autumn and finally, I could say "Follow my
hands as I have led you this way forever." And the wind, having
no memory of forever, believed that this was so and therefore
had always been so. How could it doubt I was who I claimed to
be? After all, had we not moved together and had it not now been
reminded that this had always been?
So once again I spoke, my purpose being to keep my image in its
fragile memory,
            "I have known you with whisper, shout and breath,
                Shared with you, submission and mastery,
               Shared with you the gift of motion and stillness
                    Now know and remember me!"
And the wind enveloped me and inhaled me   and

From the breath of my voice to the scent carried on the tiny hairs
between my legs, I was known!
                    quiet then
                 rocking with shivers
             head cradled between my knees
                my own steamy urine
                    trickles
                    down to
             where a bald-faced chestnut mare
                  stood watch
                  like a ghost

                     .

Mother Nature

I am blue skies
trailed with perfect black birds
over an autumnal tree line

I am an ocean so blue
it makes everything else seem white,
A forest of shadows so deep any midnight would be envious

I have been the heat from which the iron of this planet
ran.
I have been an ice so deep
that for a thousand years the sun stood in retreat.

And you with self-shackled minds,
dreams tinier than any, ever- living thing?
what you do you think pursuers of poisons?
are there any poisons that are not mine?
what do you think deniers of your own senses?
where do you think the chemicals for those thoughts come from?

I have seen stars begin and watched them dwindle.
I have seen every living thing that has ever done so,
and will see everyone that ever will be, born and die.

Do you think I who hold on to nothing care about what you do?

Maybe there is this kitchen,

there's no place left to walk
there nowhere ever to go
and whatever might need doing
sure, it'll just get undone

so maybe there is this kitchen
maybe the coffees ready
and all the sun that hasn't shined
decides to forget about winter and
hang around instead

what could I do to tell you
what could I say to show you
one day when we were not yet old
didn't we have so many things to do
and despite all that busy we still found out who we were

but now at the end of music
now close to the end of time
now that I'm just on my own
seems like loneliness is ok
some new girl on the stereo
reminding me
a few minutes
to remember
a few minutes beyond regret
you and me
once young
once upon a time

maybe you 'll come by
before it's too far gone today
I'd put more coffee on
I'd share these new tunes with you
the sun will smile even brighter
or maybe it's just
a bunch of yellow flowers in a jug
a sink of dirty dishes
an old pointer dogs silent tail wag

Through her he was to know God

she brought him inward
through a darkness full of wonder
empty of fear
she shared him mysteries
free from all that was jagged
it was not big
it was not seduction
it was an encompassing healing
a grace full of joyful weeping
silence the first breath he ever fully took her beauty communion

A Mandala of Dinosaurs, A Message of Lovers, A Mostly of Crows

A mandala of dinosaurs
A red sky of warnings
A zygote of intelligence
Soda of psychopaths
Herald of crows
An eclipse of educators
An autumn of smudges
A summer of topiaries
Empire of penises
A catapult of efforts
An envy of ravens
A coagulant of desires
Kick-start of starlings
Bucket of worms
A giggle of girls
A Saladin of wisdoms
A plague of religions
Sanctity of prisoners
Trombone of sex
A pudding of infants
A tumble of puppies
Meander of mysteries
A complaint of crows
An ignorance of drivers
A crux of sons
A delightful of crows
A moonbeam of tongues

A pestilence of motorcyclists
A coyote of marzipan
Crystal of Elan-ists
Preponderance of dictators
Kansas of superpowers
Blessing of coffees
A winter of geese
A spring of dreams
A squander of vaginas
A plethora of crows
A parcel of pachyderms
A Mercury of fish
Meandering of serpents
Sack of cats
Shyness of boys
A crisis of faiths
Carpet of breadcrumbs
A rats-ass of carers
Conglomerate of crows
A declaration of seashells
A cartoon of kittens
A half league of words
A severance of hopes
A Shenandoah of daughters
A crossing of souls
A smatter of kisses
A secretion of secrets

A message of lovers.

Useless

A lump of wood
Too big for the stove
Too small to bother with re-cutting
Weighed down the lid of the recycle barrel
Until they moved
Then someone threw it over the fence into the hedge row

The Woman

I could not speak.
Maybe loved more gently
I could have.
Maybe if there was a moon
I could have.
But only sun –
a crazy glue
unswallowed
lips sealed
slays weds
impregnates
itself.
This is what I cannot say,
this is what they refuse to hear:
After death is pre- natal.
Through me, everything is world.
Without me?
Conception is by eating,
birth by excretion.

We will surround you with silence

Like the voices of our children never to be heard again

We will surround you with fallen lilies
Like each of one our children cut mid bloom

We won't ever know what to do
With a hypocrite's thoughts and prayers
We won't ever find anything
In a hypocrite's concern for our grief

But we'll not match the hardness of such hearts
By hardening our own
We will not meet such hearts with violence
We know too well that path of sorrow

So, we will meet you in silence
Like the voices of our children never to be heard again
We will meet you in fallen lilies
Like each one of our children cut mid bloom

Unlike you
We will do what must be done

Unlike you
We will remember and continue to find days to be thankful for

Mothers rocking babies rocking mothers
Fathers rocking babies rocking fathers

Then there was Maureen in evening laughter,

Restless martial arts forms against the stars
Stoned as shit on some hashish she bought
To see her now, happy, carefree, no self-put downs,
Golden lady I like to be here…
Maureen your skin is magic,
The night has been beautiful for us
The moonless stars are animals I want to travel among
While your desire is to keep both feet on firm earth
Dancing in the dark I hate to leave you –
All night my fingers shake in their sleep as if I had ten penises
each dreaming of your cunt all at once.

Boomerz

I live only in memory.
The day to day does not inspire me,
Only wanting to sit here and think of what used to be
Strung out on the drug America.

Safe only in my own home,
Locked doors, paid taxes, insurance policies protect me.
TV-petrol- chemicals nourish me.
People not like me, outrage me

Did the Yankees still have a chance for the Pennant

Today
at the counter
pastrami on rye
coffee black
just off the peripheral
this guy and woman at a table
he was going on & on
you know right away
a bunch of bullshit
rather loudly too
I had no interest in him
or what he was selling
but she had caught my eye
noticed her the minute I came in
by the time I finished my sandwich
she still hadn't said a word
he of course hadn't stopped
people just tried to piss him off
daughter 13 years old competing already
lack of parenting by all others
ad nauseam
I asked the waitress for a refill and the check
turned to get a better look at them
maybe she was speaking, just too soft for me to hear?
but no. she was just sitting there taking it all in.
no longer interested but rather sorry for her
turned to finish my coffee
wondered how long the rain would hold off
did the Yankees still have a chance for the pennant...?

Could she but think of Cape Cod

Sand spray ridges
Heartbeat trombone ocean
still out of sight
flavours the air
her hair
and

Shifting down to the open beach
opalized lumps of stone
darker lighter sand
crazy north east gales
bit by
bit

Trail of *unnecessaries*
Shoes Coat
Shirt Skirt
Polka dot bra Unmatched panties
A string of moonish pearls returned

In favour of ice climbing

used to climb these ledges
hot summer days
high enough
thread like river
above the trees
escape the mosquitoes...
desperate for a hand hold
almost grabbed a fucking snake once

(For Martin - St. Johns Ledges, Kent)

She's a Bamboo Bitch

constantly under
someone's fingernails.
On the roof grey shingles
rain collects
finds an escape over the bed.
drop by
drop
the bamboo
grows.
Tired of a leaky
bed
I lie downstairs
on the couch
trying to see things
in the dark.
When the rain stops
it is so quiet
I think of swimming to Brazil
to tell people
I came from Surinam.
The mud will be deep.
It has rained for days.
But today
sunlight in the dawn
she's calling me
to see.

Behind

whenever she goes
she always leaves
through differing doorways
the same absence

Modern Prayers

hand cut stones
yellowed notes
empty glasses
tobacco crumbs
   What wind whispers
   What lies bleeding
machines against old houses go
this land un-held by any heart
prefers the prayers of modern times:
   Let us forget the old
   Let us forget the dead
   Let us forget
   Amen

In her glow

we sit pretending
  so many things
like we are not old
like we are not imagining
warm alabaster
against our dark skin
fiery silk her hair
between our sure and steady fingers
a scent of jasmine
through the open windows of a moonless night
all infusing
all reviving
her fire our youth
no, we are not thinking that at all

I am dead already

~ So
there is nothing really to worry about
~ Although sometimes I still forget
think of myself as living
things to do
places to go
achievements to achieve
people to please and all
eventually I come around
focus by saying
" you don't have to"
usually that's enough to bring me back to what is
~ Other times,
especially if I have forgotten for maybe days,
years, occasionally decades
it takes stuff a little stronger not much though, you know
just say out loud to my so-called self;
"you are already dead "
 helps me relax
brings me round to that expansive place of what is
a pleasant space of truth

Dreams before the growing season of grass

Not early enough
The day already begun
Anyone with any place to be
Already there or else so late it's not worth fretting about
Brand new bus, half empty
At least two hours to go

No ghosts dance over the river
No diamond tips the foliage
No dark shapes emerge

A girl you used to know
Leads a horse you used to own
Liver chestnut
White star snip
Bucks rears dares

Once your brown hands could do anything
    Melt the mouths of untried horses
    Finalise another divorce
    Set paddock posts well below the frost line
    Pull sunglasses from a girl
    Hold her surprised to kiss
    And kiss and kiss again
    As if there would never be anything else to ever do.

Rumours of another Summer

95°
4th of July
Connecticut
Bare Trees, Winter Night; Fleetwood Mac
 oldie not so familiar says the radio.

this is age
& what it's like
& how is there anything else now?

But poplar silver
still sounds like rain
quicksand springs still stream
maples shade deep gorge brooks
high stones circle the pool
of where going down to the horse bones
we were kids.

Snow

silent
soft
unable to do anything but fall
stops a millennium in its tracks

Pop_*

Down the streets of ecstasy
I take my chances endlessly
But there's no need for me to run
With my fingers wrapped around a gun

  Look around what do you see
  There ain't nothing here for me

Reality what can it be
But a misery you set for me
And there's no sense in wanting more
This is what I been put here for

You preachers of morality
How would you do to live like me?
Heavens just a novelty
Another thing denied to me.

So down the streets of ecstasy
I'll make my way most carelessly
And you can judge it tragedy
But I won't surrender easily.

* recorded by Background on All the Answers

The Lover of Wisdom

He helped in the kitchen
While she was away.
One night he was worried about the wine
Her father noticed, told him
Not to worry
They said it was the best place they'd been to
That they were glad to be here,
Besides it was the second bottle they'd ordered.
It was then he grabbed her father's hand, said
Are you my friend? Are you!
The towering man with black moustache
In a well-worn greasy apron said,
Always. I am your friend always!
It was evening when she came back.
He was sorting pots from the green house
Packing them into the jeep
Parked at the top of the driveway
When they pulled in
BMW convertible dark blue w/ tan leather.
He did not want to meet her friends.
Afraid they'd hear the beating of his heart
He stayed on the other side of the jeep
Pretending to be too busy
Waiting for her to come to him.
But after their long good-byes,
She didn't.
He walked around saw her walking
Down the hill with her bags
He thought – she has not come back at all then.

Shortly later she came back.
Sat with him on the grass
Her black hair veiling them
As hunched together head to head
He opened what she gave him
Wrapped in white tissues
A ball of crystal inside a ball of alabaster.
I missed you so much he said.
Are you brave enough to let me shave you? She said.
Come on. Let me. I want to.
He had not shaved since she left
And her creamy skin could not abide a whiskered face

Ritual

Silent on the back steps
Smoke spirals
Past heat stuck insects
Webs of spider's 60-watt bulb
Cracking whiskery grey paint
Four glass panes never meant to be opened
Stars peek in
& you come along
Not necessarily to join me
But sit beside me none the less
Nimbly roll one for yourself
& then another one for me.

(For Ulrike)

The girl next door

When I remember
third floor windows
tall white lace sails
summer all running in our veins
her mother in the kitchen
making cool aid and plate full of something
cookie sweet to eat

she wanted me to stay
I was afraid, wanted to go home
but didn't want her to know
Not wanting to be in this house of too many windows
overlooking this mill town valley

but she wanted me to stay
besides the rains begun
going to be a real storm
already rumblings from darkening horizon

and her mother agreed
I'll call your parents
They won't be worried
You can stay for supper
You like hot dogs, don't you?

and that was how I learned not to be afraid of storms
not to hide from thunder or lightning
Frances and her mother guiding me with their exuberance
ohhs ahhs joy over every menacing vibration or sudden crash
every flash or veining skeletal zig zag